Outfielder Frank Robinson

THE STORY OF THE BALTIMORE ORIOLES

Outfielder Colton Cowser

THE STORY OF THE

BALTIMORE ORIOLES

JIM WHITING

CREATIVE SPORTS

First baseman Eddie Murray

CREATIVE EDUCATION / CREATIVE PAPERBACKS

Published by Creative Education and Creative Paperbacks
P.O. Box 227, Mankato, Minnesota 56002
Creative Education and Creative Paperbacks are imprints of
The Creative Company
www.thecreativecompany.us

Book Design by Graham Morgan
Art direction by Blue Design (www.bluedes.com)

Images by Associated Press/Mark J. Terrill, 4–5, 32; Getty Images/Bettmann, 16, Bob Gomel/Time Life Pictures, 1, Diamond Images, 7 (bottom, left), Focus On Sport, 6 (bottom, left), 6 (bottom, right), 7 (top, left), 7 (top, right), 9, 10, 18, 19, 20, George Kubas/Diamond Images, 30, 31, Hy Peskin/Time Life Pictures, 15, Jamie Squire, 25, Lisa Blumenfeld, 6 (top, right), Louis DeLuca, 11, Mike Carlson, 2, National Baseball Hall of Fame Library, 7 (bottom, right), Nick Cammett/Diamond Images, cover, 29, SPX/Diamond Images, 3, 10, TED MATHIAS/AFP, cover, 22–23, Tim Umphrey, 26–27, Tony Tomsic, 6 (top, left); Wikimedia Commons/Bain News Service, publisher, 12

Library of Congress Cataloging-in-Publication Data
Names: Whiting, Jim, 1943- author
Title: The story of the Baltimore Orioles / by Jim Whiting.
Description: Mankato, Minnesota : Creative Education and Creative Paperbacks, [2026] | Series: Creative sports. Major League baseball | Includes index. | Audience: Ages 8-12 | Audience: Grades 4-6 | Summary: "Discover the Baltimore Orioles' thrilling journey from Milwaukee to Maryland, highlighting iconic players, historic wins, and the Major League Baseball team's resilience through triumphs and rebuilding phases. Written for middle-grade readers. Includes table of contents, sidebars, and index"– Provided by publisher.
Identifiers: LCCN 2025013163 (print) | LCCN 2025013164 (ebook) | ISBN 9798895810866 library binding | ISBN 9798896800392 paperback | ISBN 9798895812129 ebook
Subjects: LCSH: Baltimore Orioles (Baseball team)–History–Juvenile literature | Baltimore (Md.)–History, Local
Classification: LCC GV875.B2 W553 2026 (print) | LCC GV875.B2 (ebook) | DDC 796.357/64097526–dc23/eng/20250520
LC record available at https://lccn.loc.gov/2025013163
LC ebook record available at https://lccn.loc.gov/2025013164

Printed in the United States

Outfielder Anthony Santander

Baltimore
5
320

46

Orioles
33

BUCS
Astros
11

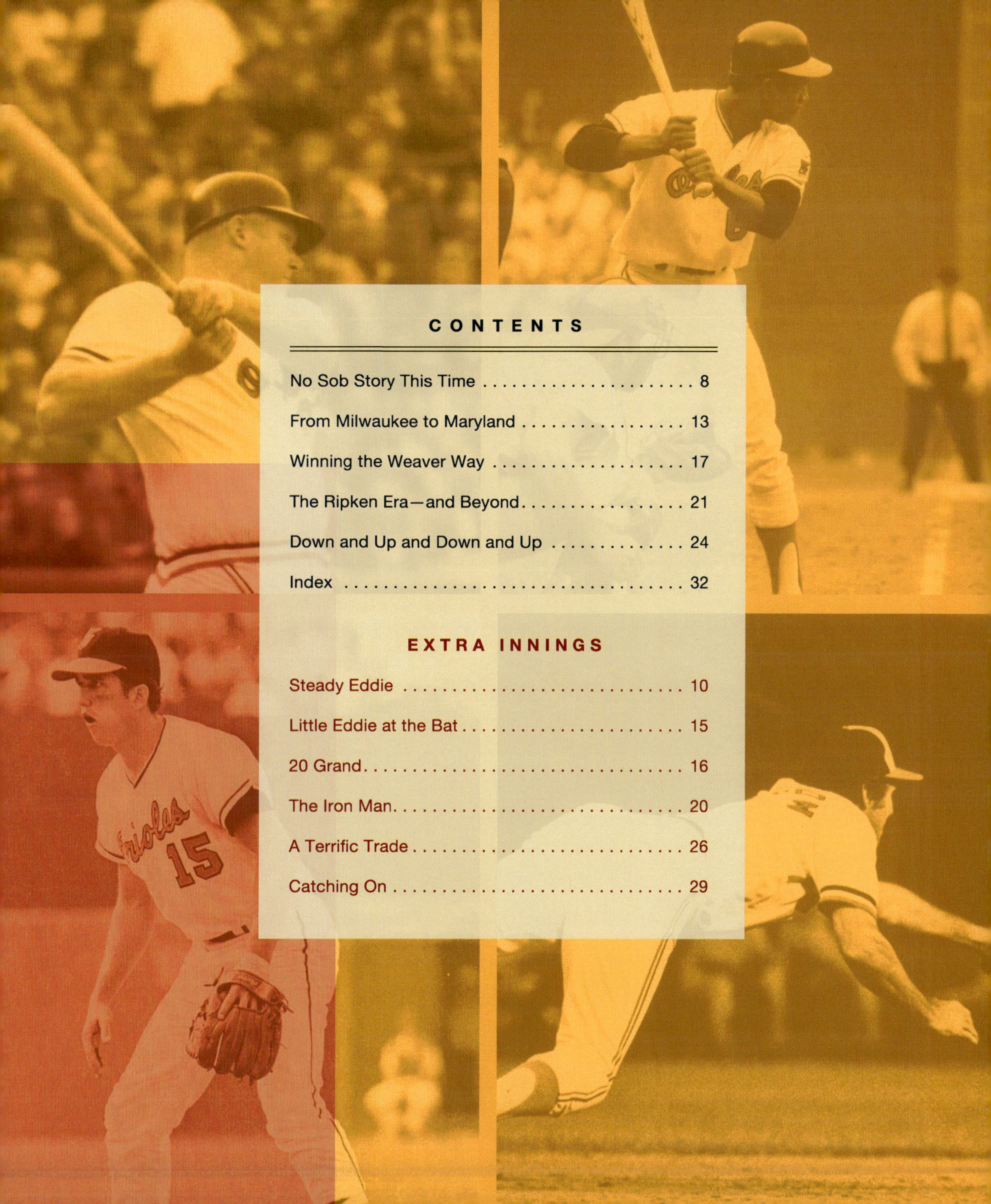

CONTENTS

EXTRA INNINGS

NO SOB STORY THIS TIME

It was two in the morning before Game 5 of the 1983 World Series between the Philadelphia Phillies and the Baltimore Orioles. Baltimore starting pitcher Scott McGregor lay on the floor of his hotel room, sobbing. He was recalling what had happened four years earlier. The Orioles had won three of the first four games in that season's World Series against the Pittsburgh Pirates. They only needed one more victory to seal the deal. They were supremely confident. "We were already designing our [championship] rings," McGregor remembered.

The mayor of Baltimore was also confident. Before Game 5, he publicly announced the parade route the Orioles would take when they returned home.

Pittsburgh used that announcement as motivation. They won the next three games to take the Series.

"After each win we joked, 'We just canceled a parade,'" Pirates pitcher Kent Tekulve said. "'Let's cancel another one.'"

Third baseman Doug DeCinces runs in the 1979 World Series.

EDDIE MURRAY
FIRST BASE
ORIOLES SEASONS: 1977–88
HEIGHT: 6-FOOT-2
WEIGHT: 190 POUNDS
KEY STATS: .294 BATTING AVERAGE, 343 HOME RUNS, 1,224 RBIS, 7X ALL-STAR

STEADY EDDIE

Eddie Murray had an immediate impact when he joined the Orioles. He played in 160 games, batting .283 and slamming 27 home runs. He was named the 1977 Rookie of the Year. Nicknamed "Steady Eddie" for his consistency at the plate and in the field, he won three straight Gold Glove awards (1982, 1983, 1984). He is just one of seven players with 3,000 hits and 500 home runs in his career. His 343 home runs are second in team history. He was voted into the Baseball Hall of Fame in 2003. "When I got to the big leagues, there was a man—Eddie Murray—who showed me how to play this game, day in and day out," said Cal Ripken Jr. "I thank him for his example."

First baseman **Eddie Murray**

The Pirates canceled the parade three times as the Baltimore bats fell silent. The Orioles scored just a single run in Game 5. The Pirates shut them out in Game 6. Baltimore scored only one run in the deciding Game 7. McGregor was the losing pitcher. It was just the fourth time in World Series history that a team had a 3–1 lead and lost the remaining three games.

Now, four years later, the Orioles had a 3–1 lead again, this time over the Phillies. As McGregor lay crying in the darkness, he thought, "We cannot be the only team in history to do this twice. We cannot get up 3–1 [and lose]."

They didn't. Game 5 started out strong as powerful Baltimore first baseman Eddie Murray slammed two home runs. Catcher Rick Dempsey added a third long ball. McGregor pitched a ball. He kept the Phillies from scoring any runs as the Orioles won 5–0.

"In 1979, we came back [to Baltimore], and there was a lot of people who came out who had a lot of tears in their eyes because we lost," Dempsey said. "This year we got tears in our eyes because we won."

And they got their victory parade. An estimated 200,000 people turned out in downtown Baltimore the next day. "It was a nice family feeling," wrote the ***Washington Post***. "Several players carried their small children."

FROM MILWAUKEE TO MARYLAND

Baltimore figures prominently in Major League Baseball (MLB) history. The legendary New York Yankees slugger Babe Ruth was born there in 1895. Six years later, the American League (AL) became a major league. One of the first teams, the Milwaukee Brewers, was not very good. Few fans attended the games. The team moved to St. Louis in 1902. It became the Browns. The team notched 78 wins. It was a 30-game improvement over the previous season. But from then on, winning was a struggle. The Browns posted just 11 winning records in the next 51 seasons.

One of the team's few good seasons came in 1922. Left fielder Ken Williams belted 39 home runs. That was four more than Ruth. The team won 93 games. But Ruth and his Yankees won the league title by a single game. In 1944, All-Star shortstop Vern Stephens helped St. Louis win the AL pennant for the first—and only—time. The Browns faced their crosstown rivals, the St. Louis Cardinals, in the World Series. The Cardinals took the championship in six games. The Browns returned to their losing ways. Attendance sagged.

In desperation, owner Bill Veeck sold the franchise to a group of Baltimore businessmen. They moved the team to Maryland for the 1954 season. They renamed it the Orioles, after Maryland's state bird. The team colors were orange and black, just like the birds. The Orioles posted a 54–100 record in their first season.

Left fielder Ken Williams

Baltimore began investing in its minor-league system to develop young players. It became known as the "Oriole Way." The first great player that the Oriole Way produced was gangly third baseman Brooks Robinson. He was a defensive wizard. In 1960, the team had a breakthrough year. Robinson batted .294. Rookie pitcher Chuck Estrada had a league-leading 18 victories. Fellow rookie shortstop Ron Hansen clubbed 22 homers. The Orioles finished 89–65. It was the team's first winning record in Baltimore.

The Orioles remained strong. In 1965, they traded three players to the Cincinnati Reds for outfielder Frank Robinson. He had been the 1961 National League (NL) Most Valuable Player (MVP). The trade was one of the best in Orioles history. In 1966, he won the AL Triple Crown with a .316 average, 49 home runs, and 122 runs batted in (RBIs). Brooks Robinson added 23 home runs and 100 RBIs. Jim Palmer and Dave McNally anchored a talented pitching staff. The Orioles clinched the AL pennant with a 97–63 record.

In the World Series, Baltimore faced the Los Angeles Dodgers. In Game 1, both Robinsons slugged home runs. The Orioles won, 5–2. Baltimore rolled to a four-game sweep. It was the franchise's first world championship. "To do that to a ballclub as good as the Dodgers is almost unthinkable," said Brooks Robinson. "I'm just glad I was here to see it."

EXTRA INNINGS

LITTLE EDDIE AT THE BAT

Browns owner Bill Veeck was notorious for publicity stunts. One of the most outrageous came when newly signed Eddie Gaedel stepped up to the plate as a pinch hitter in the bottom of the first inning. What made the substitution notable was that Gaedel stood only 3-foot-7! Tigers pitcher Bob Cain laughed as he prepared to pitch to the tiniest strike zone in MLB history. Not surprisingly, Gaedel walked on four pitches. A pinch runner replaced him at first base. He left to a standing ovation. AL president Will Harridge voided Gaedel's contract the next day. It is the shortest career in MLB history.

DETROIT TIGERS VS.
ST. LOUIS BROWNS
AUGUST 19, 1951

EXTRA INNINGS

PITCHING ACES (LEFT TO RIGHT) DAVE MCNALLY (19), JIM PALMER (22), AND MIKE CUELLAR (35)

20 GRAND

In 1970 and 1971, the Orioles had one of the most dominant back-to-back pitching rotations in MLB history. In 1970, Mike Cuellar and Dave McNally both won 24 games. Flamethrower Jim Palmer added 20 more. He threw 199 strikeouts, too. The Orioles topped the AL with 108 victories. They went on to win the World Series. The next year, McNally led the staff with 21 wins. Cuellar and Palmer each threw 20. New addition Pat Dobson made 1971 even better. He also hurled 20 victories. The Orioles joined the 1920 Chicago White Sox as the only teams with four 20-game winning pitchers.

WINNING THE WEAVER WAY

Baltimore declined in 1967. It won just 76 games. Midway through the 1968 season, manager Hank Bauer was fired. Earl Weaver replaced him. Baltimore's feisty new skipper lit a fire under the Orioles. Weaver summed up his style as "pitching, defense, and the three-run homer." He did not believe in "small ball," and its emphasis on stolen bases, hit-and-run plays, and sacrifice bunts. The Orioles finished second in the American League with 91 wins. But at that time, only the league champions advanced to the post-season.

The AL split into two divisions in 1969. The Orioles stormed through the regular season in the AL East Division. They finished with a franchise-record 109 victories. The Robinsons continued to provide offensive power. The booming bat of first baseman Boog Powell helped out. So did speedy center fielder Paul Blair. Shortstop Mark Belanger and second baseman Davey Johnson provided Gold Glove-winning defense. The Orioles swept the Minnesota Twins in three games in the AL Championship Series (ALCS), which matched the division winners. Baltimore faced the New York Mets in the World Series. The Orioles were heavily favored. But the "Miracle Mets" upset Baltimore in five games.

Stung by the loss, the Orioles came out swinging in 1970. They went 108–54. Baltimore again topped the AL East. It again defeated the Twins in the ALCS. The team headed back to the World Series. There, it faced the mighty Cincinnati Reds. Brooks Robinson put on a jaw-dropping defensive show. He also batted .429 with two home runs and six RBIs. The Orioles beat the Reds in

Brooks Robinson and Mike Cuellar celebrate after winning Game 5 the World Series.

five games. "Baseball is a team game," said Weaver, "but what Brooks did is as close as I've ever seen one player come to winning a series by himself."

The following year, the Orioles won 101 games. That propelled them to a third consecutive World Series. This time they met the Pittsburgh Pirates. There would be no championship repeat. The Pirates won the deciding Game 7 with a 2–1 score.

The Orioles captured division titles in 1973 and 1974. But they lost the ALCS each time. By 1978, the team had changed dramatically. Most of its big hitters were gone.

A new generation of Orioles stepped up. Eddie Murray was among the best first basemen in the game. Speedy outfielder Al Bumbry was a base-stealing marvel. Third baseman Doug DeCinces was a heavy hitter. Outfielders John Lowenstein and Ken Singleton also provided plenty of power. Mike Flanagan and Dennis Martínez led the team's pitching staff. These new Orioles compiled a 102–57 record in 1979. The team was back atop the AL East. It defeated the Los Angeles Angels in the ALCS. Then Baltimore faced the Pirates in the World Series. The Pirates came back from a 3–1 deficit to win the series in seven games.

Third baseman Brooks Robinson

CAL RIPKEN JR.
SHORTSTOP
ORIOLES SEASONS: 1981–2001
HEIGHT: 6-FOOT-4
WEIGHT: 200 POUNDS
KEY STATS: .276 BATTING AVERAGE, 431 HOME RUNS, 1,695 RBIS, 13X ALL-STAR

THE IRON MAN

Cal Ripken Jr. trotted onto the field at Baltimore's Memorial Stadium on May 30, 1982. None of the 21,632 fans paid much attention as he grounded out and struck out. The scene was vastly different on September 6, 1995. A crowd of 46,272 people packed Oriole Park at Camden Yards. Ripken was the center of attention. Ever since that lackluster day in 1982, Ripken had played in every Orioles game. His streak was now 2,131. That broke the record set by New York Yankees first baseman Lou Gehrig. Fans had thought Gehrig's record was unbreakable. Ripken took his accomplishment in stride. "It was very simple. I wanted to come to the ballpark, I wanted to play, I wanted to help the team win."

THE RIPKEN ERA—AND BEYOND

In 1982, Orioles fans witnessed a passing of the torch from one Baltimore icon to another. Weaver finished his 16-year managing stint as shortstop Cal Ripken Jr. completed his first full MLB season. Baltimore finished second in the AL East, just one game behind the Milwaukee Brewers. In 1983, the team rolled to the AL East title with a 98–64 record. It defeated the Chicago White Sox to win the AL pennant. Baltimore went on to win the World Series. "We have always relied on our pitchers," noted catcher Rick Dempsey. "When you can roll out guys like Palmer, Flanagan, and McGregor every day, you're going to win a lot of games."

After that championship, the Orioles experienced a gradual decline. The once-stellar pitching staff began to fall apart. Baltimore set an MLB record when it began the 1988 season with 21 straight losses. Nevertheless, Ripken consistently gave strong performances. Newcomers such as outfielder Brady Anderson and dominating pitcher Mike Mussina did well, too. But as a team, the Orioles struggled.

In 1992, the team moved into a new baseball-only facility, Oriole Park at Camden Yards. Many MLB teams played in huge multi-purpose ballparks surrounded by vast parking lots. Oriole Park at Camden Yards changed that. It is a throwback to an earlier era that fits into its neighborhood. Inspired by their new nest, the Orioles enjoyed three straight winning seasons.

The Orioles added veteran slugging first baseman Rafael Palmeiro in 1994. Baltimore was near the top of the division. But a players' strike in August ended the season early. There were no playoffs. The team finished third in 1995. Led by Ripken, Palmeiro, Anderson, and sure-handed second baseman

RIPKEN
8

Shortstop Cal Ripken Jr.

Roberto Alomar, the team won the division in both 1996 and 1997. But it lost the ALCS both times.

The 1998 season marked the beginning of a new era for the Orioles. The organization had fallen into the habit of signing expensive free agents. The team ended up with a huge payroll and few young impact players. It would be an uphill battle to return to the top of the division.

In the midst of the team's slide, Ripken continued to shine. He surpassed 400 home runs in 1999. He made it to 3,000 hits the following year. Ripken became only the seventh major-leaguer to achieve both marks. He retired in 2001. "Cal's retirement brings an end to one of the finest, most noble careers this game has ever seen," said Brooks Robinson.

By then, Orioles fans had suffered through four straight losing seasons. The win total declined every year. Fans had high hopes in 2004. The Orioles acquired hot-hitting catcher Javy López and smooth shortstop Miguel Tejada. The additions paid immediate dividends. López hit .316 and bashed 23 home runs. Tejada led the major leagues with 150 RBIs. Yet Baltimore finished 78–84. "This is a good, good ballclub," manager Lee Mazzilli insisted. "This is a club that can compete with any team in the league."

DOWN AND UP AND DOWN AND UP

Mazzilli was wrong. The team won just 74 games in 2005 and 70 in 2006. After that, the Orioles failed to even reach 70 wins for the next five years. Their losing streak stretched to 14 seasons. But as All-Star outfielder Adam Jones explained, "[Baltimore]

Shortstop Miguel Tejada

Oriole
31

ADAM JONES
CENTER FIELD
ORIOLES SEASONS: 2008–18
HEIGHT: 6-FOOT-2
WEIGHT: 215 POUNDS
KEY STATS: .319 BATTING AVERAGE, 263 HOME RUNS, 945 RBIS, 5X ALL-STAR

A TERRIFIC TRADE

Getting Adam Jones by a trade with the Seattle Mariners was one of the best moves in Baltimore history. Jones had an immediate impact with his new team. He became an All-Star in just his second season. Jones was a durable player who played in nearly every game. As Jake Rill of mlb.com wrote, "The max effort on a nightly basis. Adam Jones was the heart and soul of an entire generation of Orioles baseball." He had seven straight seasons with at least 25 home runs, which helped place him fifth all-time in franchise history. He was also an outstanding fielder. He won Gold Glove awards in 2009, 2012, 2013, and 2014.

EXTRA INNINGS

has been kind of the hidden city over the last decade . . . It's young and raw, but I think we have a very good team." Unlike Mazzilli, Jones was right.

Baltimore confounded expectations in 2012. The Orioles flipped their 2011 record of 69–93 to 93–69. The Orioles made their first playoff appearance in 15 years. They beat the Texas Rangers 5–1 in the Wild Card game. They took on the Yankees in the ALDS. But New York prevailed, three games to two. The following season, first baseman Chris Davis led the major leagues with 53 home runs. Still, the 85–77 Orioles fell short of the playoffs.

In 2014, Baltimore tallied a 96–66 mark. It won the AL East for the first time since 1997. The team swept the Detroit Tigers in the ALDS. But the Kansas City Royals swept the Orioles in the ALCS. After ending the following season 81–81, the Orioles rebounded to win 89 games in 2016. The key was an exceptional bullpen. Closer Zach Britton had 47 saves and a microscopic 0.54 earned run average (ERA). The team played in the Wild Card game against the Toronto Blue Jays. Toronto used a three-run walk-off home run in the 11th inning to win.

During this five-season run of success, the Orioles won more games than any other AL team. Baltimore appeared to be on a roll at the start of the 2017 season. It began 22–10. But the team stumbled the rest of the way. It was still in the Wild Card race in early September. After a 4–19 finish, the team's overall record was a disappointing 75–87 and out of the playoffs.

That set the stage for a dismal 2018. The team traded some of its best players in an effort to rebuild. It won just 47 games while losing 115, the second-worst season in team history. Baltimore was a whopping 61 games behind the division-leading Boston Red Sox. The bad times continued in 2019. The Orioles finished 54–108. Yet again, they finished at the bottom of the AL East. After finishing 25–35 in the COVID-19-shortened 2020 season, Baltimore went just 52–110 in 2021.

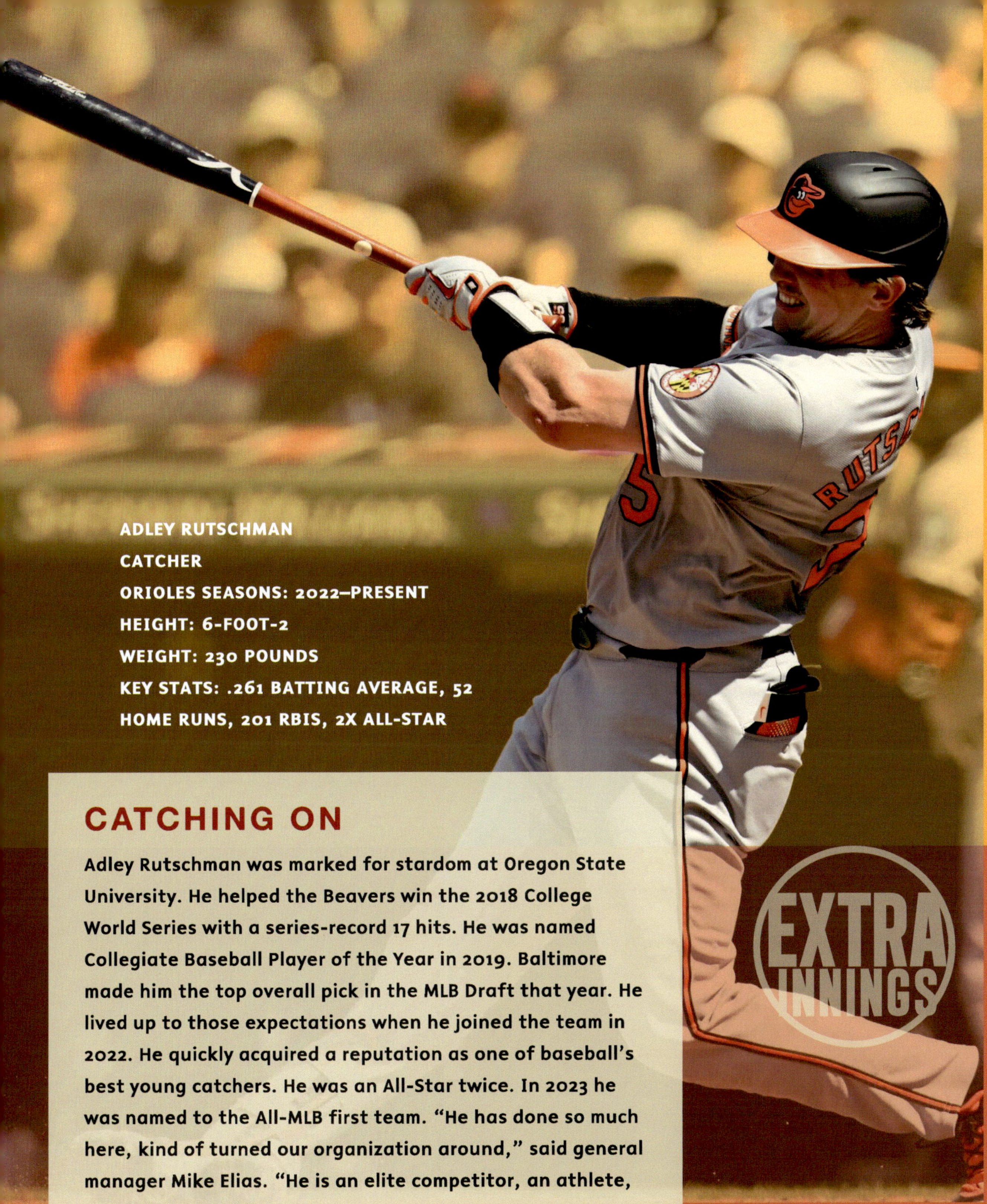

ADLEY RUTSCHMAN
CATCHER
ORIOLES SEASONS: 2022–PRESENT
HEIGHT: 6-FOOT-2
WEIGHT: 230 POUNDS
KEY STATS: .261 BATTING AVERAGE, 52 HOME RUNS, 201 RBIS, 2X ALL-STAR

EXTRA INNINGS

CATCHING ON

Adley Rutschman was marked for stardom at Oregon State University. He helped the Beavers win the 2018 College World Series with a series-record 17 hits. He was named Collegiate Baseball Player of the Year in 2019. Baltimore made him the top overall pick in the MLB Draft that year. He lived up to those expectations when he joined the team in 2022. He quickly acquired a reputation as one of baseball's best young catchers. He was an All-Star twice. In 2023 he was named to the All-MLB first team. "He has done so much here, kind of turned our organization around," said general manager Mike Elias. "He is an elite competitor, an athlete, and he's our guy."

Catcher Adley Rutschman

It was a different story in 2022. Baltimore went 83–79. It was their first winning season since 2016. The 31-game win differential was one of the largest in MLB history. One reason for the dramatic improvement was rookie catcher Adley Rutschman. He provided stability behind the plate and was runner-up for Rookie of the Year honors. While the team missed the playoffs, it set the stage for a stellar 2023. The 101–61 mark won the East Division. Third baseman Gunnar Henderson was named Rookie of the Year. But the Orioles lost the ALDS to the Rangers, three games to none.

Though Baltimore fell back to 91–71 in 2024, they returned to the playoffs. They lost the Wild Card Series to the Royals, 2–0.

Baltimore has had many good teams in its long history. Through 2024, seven made it to the World Series. Three hoisted the World Series trophy, baseball's greatest prize. As the Orioles take flight each season in Camden Yards, fans look forward to the day when orange and black will be championship colors again.

Third baseman Gunnar Henderson

INDEX